THE UNINHIBITED MIND

Breakthrough Strategies to Achieve a Higher Level Thinking, Learning, Memory, and Performance

Jonathan S. Walker

Copyright © 2017 Jonathan S. Walker

All rights reserved.

DEDICATION

I dedicate this book as well to my two beautiful children and my loving wife who have been nothing short of being my light and joy throughout the years.

Table of Contents

Part 1

Introduction

Chapter 1: Learning About Memory

Chapter 2: Thinking and Problem Solving

Chapter 3: Learning and Attention Performance

Part 2

Chapter 1: Health Benefits of Decluttering

Chapter 2: Joys of Simple Living

Chapter 3: Clutter Overhaul

Chapter 4: 5 Minute Daily Declutter

Chapter 5: Organization 101

Part 3

Chapter 1: Different Emotions and How to Handle Them

Chapter 2: Meditation for Emotion

Chapter 3: Self-discipline

Conclusion

Copyright 2017 by Jonathan S. Walker - All rights reserved.

The following eBook is reproduced below with the goal of providing information that is as accurate and reliable as possible. Regardless, purchasing this eBook can be seen as consent to the fact that both the publisher and the author of this book are in no way experts on the topics discussed within and that any recommendations or suggestions that are made herein are for entertainment purposes only. Professionals should be consulted as needed prior to undertaking any of the action endorsed herein.

This declaration is deemed fair and valid by both the American Bar Association and the Committee of Publishers Association and is legally binding throughout the United States.

Furthermore, the transmission, duplication or reproduction of any of the following work including specific information will be considered an illegal act irrespective of if it is done electronically or in print. This extends to creating a secondary or tertiary copy of the work or a recorded copy and is only allowed with express written consent from the Publisher. All additional right reserved.

The information in the following pages is broadly considered to be a truthful and accurate account of facts and as such any inattention, use or misuse of the information in question by the reader will render any resulting actions solely under their purview. There are no scenarios in which the publisher or the original author of this work can be in any fashion deemed liable for any hardship or damages that may befall them after undertaking information described herein.

Additionally, the information in the following pages is intended only for informational purposes and should thus be thought of as universal. As befitting its nature, it is presented without assurance regarding its prolonged validity or interim quality. Trademarks that are mentioned are done without written consent and can in no way be considered an endorsement from the trademark holder.

••••

VIP Subscriber List

Dear Reader, If you would like to receive latest tips and tricks on internet marketing, exclusive strategies, upcoming books & promotions, and more, do subscribe to my mailing list in the link below! I will be giving away a free book that you can download right away as well after you subscribe to show my appreciation!

Here's the link: http://bit.do/jonathanswa

....

Introduction

In each chapter, you will learn about the processes that happen in your mind with each thing you want to improve on. Some things do not have tips on how to improve, you just have to find what works for you based on your new found understanding of the subject. Those that can be improved in some way have helpful tips attached.

Enjoy this book and best of luck on your journey to an Uninhibited Mind.

Chapter 1: Learning About Memory

The best way to improve your memory is to understand how it works.

Memory is the space in the mind where information is stored, and used from there. It can be encoded and decoded all from the one area of the brain that controls it.

Imagine that memory is a library of all the information that you have ever encountered in your life. Libraries often have rotating books. Your memory as well has rotating information. Just like libraries, the information that is rotated is based on the importance of said information.

For example, if you are not going to see a person ever again, you will only need to know their name for the duration of the conversation you are having with them, and then you don't need to remember it any further. This would use your short term memory. However, if you work with someone every day, you would need to know their name for a long amount of time. Therefore, you would commit their name to your long-term memory.

There are two forms of memory. The first form, which is called declarative, is where you physically commit something to memory. If you see something that you deem is important, you make yourself remember. Example, repeating a phone number in your head several times until you remember it.

Then there is a non-declarative memory. This is the memory you have no recollection of trying to remember. There are some things that your brain subconsciously remembers, such as street names as you pass by them.

Memory can be sometimes faulty. It is not perfect. There are lots of factors and variables that affect your memory such as the attention you provide to your different stimulus when trying to remember something and the amount of important you see on something.

Your long-term memory may fade over time if a memory has not been called upon in a while. Just as an old photograph fades, so do memories. You may find you forget how a loved one's voice sounds when they have been gone for a long time, for example.

Sensory memory

Sensory memory is a memory that is tied to your senses. Pretty much self-explanatory. However, there is more to it than that. This memory is often only committed to short term memory.

There are three types of sensory memories. There are the memories from sight, hearing, and haptic, which has to deal with touch and taste, and smell. Scientists do not know why touch, smell, and taste use the same memory functions, but they do. Hearing seems to be the most rapidly decaying in memory, while haptic seems to commit almost instantly to long term memory.

Short-term memory

Can be used alongside the term working memory. This is your memory that remembers something for a short amount of time, and then forgets it. The memories that are forgotten are often quickly are ones that are not important. Such as things you pass in a store, or someone you see on the street.

Short term memory seems to react the most to auditory stimuli. This means that when you hear something, it can be harder to forget it than when you see it.

Long-term memory

Long term memory is where you remember things for an indefinite period of time. It can decay over time. However, some things may stick with a person forever. It seems like haptic memories stay with a person the longest, even after hearing and sight memories have faded.

Long-term memory is recorded episodically and semantically, unlike the auditory fashion in which the short-term memory is recorded. This means that people may have a hard time remembering sounds over time, but they can remember things they have seen, and patterns they have noticed. Long-term memory is a bit of a mystery even to this day on how it works exactly because everyone remembers things differently.

The type of memory most people work on is their long term memory. This takes a lot of work to build up because you really cannot fight DNA. However, you can delay the onset of memory issues by strengthening your memory.

Diet

The first thing that you should work on is your diet. If you have a poor diet, then you are going to have too much fat stored in your body. Your memory relies on your body burning rather than storing fat. This is because the ketones that are created when you burn fat are essential for the creation of memory. Ketones are pretty much brain food.

To keep ketones burning, you should try the ketogenic diet. This is where you eat fewer carbs and more fat and protein to put your body in a state of ketosis. Ketosis is where you are constantly burning ketones in your body. The ketogenic diet also helps fight Alzheimer Disease. Here is some more information about the keto diet.

- **What is it?**

The Ketogenic diet, which is often shortened to just being called the keto diet, is a diet that is very high in fat, and low in carbs. It is proven to be a successful diet and is linked to helping prevent or even subside several health conditions, such as diabetes, epilepsy, and even Alzheimer's. This diet is used all around the world and will change what you thought you knew about carbs and fats.

This diet is obtained by drastically reducing one's carb intake. You replace the carbs that you would have eaten with fats, which makes your body focus on burning the fats that you are consuming and moving on the fats in your body. This process is known as ketosis, which puts the body into a constant fat burning state. It also burns ketones in your liver. This is how this diet combats

Alzheimer's. Ketones increase brain function, and supply healthier blood to the brain, to keep the person sharp as a tack, and ready to remember, and think, about anything.

This diet also reduces blood sugar and insulin levels, so it is great if you have diabetes, or are pre-diabetic. By following this diet, if you have type two diabetes, you could actually reduce the effects of your condition, and get it under control, to the point where you may not need your medicine as often.

This diet started out in the medicinal world in the nineteen twenties. It has been around for a long time but was only recently brought to public light. It started out as an effective treatment for people with epilepsy. That's right, it began as a diet to help ease the problems from seizures, and help people control their lives. It was kind of overshadowed for a while, however, as other technologies came into play, and new medicines were introduced, but once it was determined that the medicine did not help over thirty percent of patients, the diet was reintroduced into the medical field, and brought back into popularity in helping epileptic people gain some semblance of normalcy back into their lives.

- **How Does It Work?**

Your body needs calories to run. There are three types of calories. The calories that you get from protein, carbs, and fat. You want to make sure that you are getting most of your calories from fat. However, not just any fat. You want to get your calories from unsaturated fats, as these are the ones that burn ketones in your liver. Saturated fats are harder to burn, and do not send your body into ketosis.

You want to also make sure you are eating protein as well, as this helps your body stay strong throughout the day as it is filling as well. Without carbs, you may find that your body tries to go on a hunger strike, so make sure that you are eating plenty of protein as well. Protein also has a good fat content as well.

Keep your carbs under a hundred grams a day. A few carbs are okay, just try to eat twice as much protein and fat.

The keto diet is literally a diet in which you switch one type of calorie with another. In this case, you are switching carbs with fats, and even though it seems counter-intuitive, it is actually quite genius. You figure out how much you are consuming by counting your calories via macronutrients, which are the sections of calories that you need to have a balanced diet.

Exercise

Exercise actually helps keep your mind sharp, because it also helps you burn fat and keep your body in ketosis. You do not have to get an expensive gym membership; thirty minutes a day of light cardio should do the trick as well.

The more you exercise, however, the more fat you burn. The more fat you burn, the stronger your memory will get. The ketones you will be burning in your liver will help your brain function and keep your mind sharp.

Plus, exercise is a great time to think about things through the day. You can try to recall a memory from that day, and see how much you remember. This game is great for those who want to be able to remember their day with ease.

Reduce Stress

Have you ever been so stressed that you felt like you could not remember anything? Stress is known to affect your memory by causing you to focus only on what you are stressed about. This leads to you forgetting important things because your brain is not able to pay attention.

Play Memory Games

It may seem silly, but those matching memory games are really good for your visual memory. You know, the ones that you played as a little kid where you flipped a card over and tried to match it with another card by remembering the placement of that card? This game is good for you well into adulthood as it helps keep your memory sharp.

You can also play auditory memory games. There are several that have you listen to a sound, and then they show you something, and you have to remember the sound after seeing a picture that is unrelated to the sound. This is great for your auditory memory.

There are not many haptic memory games, however, because haptic senses are harder to create a game. Especially if the game is on a computer.

You can find a lot of these games online for free, so don't hesitate to check them out!

Chapter 2: Thinking and Problem Solving

Thought is viewed to be abstract. There is no real way to track how it works, as not everyone thinks in the same fashion. Even scans show the differences in parts of the brain that are used when thinking.

However, it is important to know how to keep your train of thought and strengthen your mind to focus better. This will be touched upon in the next chapter.

When you are thinking, it allows you to process the information you are taking in. If you were not to think, you would only act, and that could cause a lot of issues.

Psychology

Thought is designed to help people figure out

what they are going to do before they try to do it. It is seen as an evolutionary aspect, as humans are the only ones to think before doing anything. Perhaps it was for species preservation, but no one truly knows. It is all theories at this point.

However, there are ways you can improve your ability to think things through if that is what you are looking to do. This is the only way that has been proven to improve your thought, and it is something that a lot of people groan about when they come across it. Problem-solving.

Use Problem Solving.

Have you ever found yourself in a difficult

situation, and you are not sure where to turn? Have you found yourself wondering how to solve a certain problem? Do you often question your ability to think things through clearly? Don't fret, because you are not alone. Millions of people struggle with the ability to problem solve. However, there are ways to improve your skills.

You may be wondering what problem-solving has to do with thinking, and the answer is simple: Problem-solving forces you to use the power of thought to open your mind to the answer that may not be out in the open. By working on your problem-solving skills, you exercise your brain, which has been proven to help people think more clearly and helps them organize the thoughts that run through their mind.

Definition

Problem-solving comes with different definitions. However, at this moment, the one we will be using here is the one that is referring to common human problem-solving, not the computerized and digital problem-solving. We will define problem-solving as an act of finding out a solution to difficult, usually confusing, situations by analyzing multiple steps and by going through a process to defeat or overcome an obstacle.

Problem-solving strategies

Problem-solving, in the simplest form, is viewed as a cycle. The process goes like this: you analyze the problem, think deeply for a solution, try the solution, modify the errors, and then get the solution for the problem. And then, you have to start all over again when there is a new problem that will arise. We may not notice it, but we're doing this every day such as when deciding what to wear, searching a detour around a construction area on our way to office or work, and thinking about what we will have for lunch or dinner.

There are many different ways to look at problem-solving. If you are a math person, problem-solving probably comes to you best in mathematical form. If you are a science person, you probably approach it like the scientific method.

There is no tried and true method of improving your skills. However, there are several that are known to help, and trying them can't hurt. You are bound to find something that works for you. If you don't, that alone could be a test of your problem-solving skills, and you could try to find what works for you!

Tips for Improving Your Problem Solving Skills.

1. Dance

"There is no way dancing could in any way affect your brain." If you think this statement is true, you would be absolutely incorrect. Dancing is a great way to work on your problem-solving skills. Have you ever tried to dance? You have to coordinate each step to the beat of the music, and if you have a particularly difficult transition, then you have to figure out the best way to move through it without tripping yourself up. It is also great exercise, which is good for the brain.

Dancing burns ketones in your liver, which functions as food for your brain. This will help you brainstorm like a pro, and really get to show off what that brain of yours can do.

2. Work out Your Brain

"Logic games are for children. Adults are too old to play silly games." Another incorrect statement. Logic games stimulate your brain and help exercise it. You see, your brain is a muscle as well as an organ, and if you do not exercise it, it begins to get weak. Logic games help keep your mind sharp, and they can be fun as well. There is nothing childish about being on top of your mental strength.

It is important to exercise your brain, along with your body to really give yourself the best chance at having a strong mind to amp up your thought processes.

3. Put on the Tunes and Move

"Music is a distraction, and will get in the way." Look at us, clearing up misconceptions one myth at a time. It is actually scientifically proven that music helps stimulate brain function. That coupled with exercise is a double threat and thinking about a difficult problem to make it a triple threat.

Although physical workouts can help you think more focused and get your blood flowing to your brain, it still does not necessarily help you solve a problem, nor it improves your skills in problem-solving. However, when you add music to your exercise, you add another thing in the background which forces your mind to focus more. Thus, music can help you increase and improve your problem-solving skills significantly.

Even if you are not working out, put on some music and try to do some logic puzzles. The music will pull your mind in a different direction, making it harder for you to concentrate, thus strengthening your problem-solving skills that much more efficiently.

4. Keeping a journal

"Only teenage girls keep journals." Misconceptions everywhere. The truth is, some of the most renowned scientists and intellectuals keep journals in order to organize their often eccentric thoughts. It is impossible to remember every fleeting thought that passes through your mind, but if you write them down, you don't have to.

Journals are great for brainstorming as well. You can jot down all of your ideas that you are having and be able to pick the best one by comparing them. This is a great problem-solving tool.

6. Distance yourself from the problem

"If I am distant from a problem, it will be harder to solve." This is the opposite of correct. When you are too close to a problem, you create a barrier between the solution and your own mind. You have to take a step back so you can look at it from all angles.

It can be hard to look at a personal problem objectively. However, if you get too caught up in the problem, it can make it harder to find the best solution, because you will be biased about what to do or say to get the problem fixed. While in the long run, you may fix the problem, you can overlook a smarter and more efficient way to finish it up.

Chapter 3: Learning and Attention Performance

You know the phrase "you learn something new every day"? It is honestly true. Every day you take in new information, and that is exactly what learning is. Learning is the act of taking in information that has already been processed. You can learn through play, teaching or rote. However, teaching is actually the least effective way to learn. Many people have to experience the information first hand.

People learn in a way that is far different than animals do. While animals learn from extensive training, human learn mostly through education. Someone would teach them what he or she needs to know. Commonly, learning occurs outside the comfort of the home.

Rote learning

One of the most common ways that humans learn is through rote learning. This is the act of memorizing something. There is a special way you go about memorizing the information though. You have to write it down, say it, and see the information. The idea is that the more you handle the information, the more you will remember.

Not everyone learns the same way, which makes it difficult to pinpoint a specific way to help you learn with ease. However, improving your attention span will help increase your learning abilities a bit, as you will be able to focus more on the information you are learning.

A lot of people have a hard time focusing, so they find that they have to work harder to get their work done. However, there are ways to improve your attention span and focus, and here are some tips.

How to Improve Your Attention Span and Focus

Many people struggle day in and day out with being able to focus on their daily tasks properly. If you are one of these people, you are not alone, and there are other people in the world who are going through the same problem. In fact, over eighty percent of the world's population has trouble concentrating from time to time in varying degrees.

Some people have problems focusing daily, while others tend only to have problems if they have a lot on their plates. No matter the reason, you can beat the distractions and regain laser-like focus just by knowing how it works, and have some tips on how to keep yourself on track.

Environment

If you are in an office space. Chances are your surroundings are very boring. Some people can work well in boring scenery, and others need something to break the monotony to keep their mind from wandering. Even if you can work in a boring workstation, personalizing your space a bit may boost your morale on days where you are a little stressed, thus allowing you to leave your stress behind and work harder and focus better.

- Be comfortable: If you need to bring in your own office chair, do so. Comfort is the number one contributor and detractor for focus. You have to be comfortable so that you do not constantly have to break concentration to move around. If you are comfortable, you will be able to focus well, as you do not have to move at all.

- Add pictures: Pictures can break up the monotony of your boring space. If you are a college student, your desk is probably where you spend your life learning, so why not adorn the walls around it with some motivational landscapes or some pictures of things you enjoy. This will break the monotony and give you something to look at to keep your mind from wandering. Just stay away from pictures that have words as those can be distracting.

- Detour the noise: earplugs, earphones, and other sound canceling objects are a gift from heaven. These things keep you concentrating on your work, rather than the world around you. If you are in a noisy environment, try putting on some headphones and playing some classical music to drown out the world around you. Classical music is great to help you learn because it opens your mind. Try it out sometime.

Nutrition

The famous mantra says you are what you eat. What you put into your digestive system will affect your ability to focus. Your diet plays a huge role in your brain's functionality. If your brain does not receive the proper nutrition it needs, then it will not function properly as it should.

- Drink water: Your brain needs you to stay hydrated in order for it to properly function. If you are dehydrated, it makes it harder for you to focus, because your brain is starting to shut down to preserve itself. If you don't drink enough water, it is equivalent to literally drying out your brain. If you don't think that sounds scary, I am not sure what would scare you.

- Eat breakfast: Have you ever been really hungry? Did it make you have a hard time focusing? Hunger is one of the largest focus detractors there are. Your body needs food to function, and as a defense, when you get to a certain point food becomes all you can think about. It is best to start your day off right with a balanced breakfast so your body can make it to lunch and your mind can stay on track.

- Get up and move around: Digestion of food can be an uncomfortable process, so don't be afraid to aid it by moving. This will also help get more blood flowing to your brain. While moving around too much can distract you, taking a quick walk will help you get your mind clear and ready to learn.

Mindset

Mind over matter is another way to handle

focus difficulties. Even if you have a problem with concentrating due to a disorder, you can still improve your focus by taking control of your mind. This will allow you to focus more than you ever thought was possible.

- *Set aside time to deal with worries*: Worrying and anxiety is the number one killer of productivity. Worrying too much can kill your thoughts throughout the day, making focusing tedious and wearisome. Later in this book, we will learn how to balance work and homelife that will help you focus better.

- *Focus on one task at a time*: This may seem to go against everything that you know. However, the truth is, it is harder to learn when you are multitasking. This is because your focus is divided amongst different things, and you cannot truly give your undivided attention to what you need to be focusing on primarily. Focusing on one task at a time will help you absorb more information from the subjects you are trying to learn.

- *Close your email box and chat program*: When you are trying to learn new material, it can be tempting to take that time to also answer messages from people you know. However, that detracts from the time you have to learn what you are trying to learn. Shut down the phone, and turn off your notifications on your laptop. Just focus on the task at hand. If you take the time to really focus on what you are learning, you will find you absorb so much more information.

- *Prioritize*: Not know what to do next can kill your focus because it will eat your time figuring out what task to do next. It will stress your brain to remember things that you should not miss or forget. To avoid this, spend a little time in the morning to plan ahead your day. Make a list of what needs to prioritize and how to finish each task.

- *Switch between high- and low-priority tasks*: Many people prioritize their tasks at work from high to low. They work on the more important projects and leave the low-priority projects for last. This might seem effective for some people, but it can actually bog you down causing your brain to lose focus when starting to work on the projects that have low importance. By alternating high and low tasks, you give your brain a break making you focus longer. Thus, it will allow you to finish tasks in less time.

More Tips for Improving Your Concentration

- *Take short breaks*: Have you ever had cram session, and then found that you couldn't remember a thing you read. This is actually a pretty common occurrence. Your brain needs time to rest. Just like with a machine, sometimes you have to give it time to cool down. They can't run 24/7. You are only human. Give yourself a schedule where you study for an hour and take a five to ten-minute break. This will allow your brain to rest and reset so you can retain more information.

- *Do your hardest tasks when you're most alert*: Don't save that cram session for last minute before the big test. Do your bulk studying after breakfast. This is when your brain is typically the most alert, and you have the best chance to remember everything you studied. Saving these study sessions for when you are so tired all you can think about is sleep will kill your memory and make it harder to learn.

- Look busy: Find something that will make you look busy. Perhaps put a do not disturb sign up or wear a phone headset. This way people will know not to disturb you. If you look like you are busy, many people will wait until you are not busy to ask you a question, which allows you to learn in peace.

- Promise yourself a reward: Self-rewards is a great way to stay motivated to focus. It can be simple such as work for an hour and get a snack from the vending machine if you are successful. The trick is to hold yourself accountable if you do not meet your goal. No goal, no reward.

- Schedule email downloads: The reality is, emails do come in, for unknown reasons, at the most inconvenient times. This may be common, but it can actually distract your focus especially when you get tempted to check the emails constantly. If so, you should set a time within your day to answer emails. Once you set on a specific schedule, train yourself to download emails only at that specific period of time.

Think of Your Mind as a Muscle

Your mind is not just a typical body organ. It is also a working muscle, an essential one. It can work with heavy workloads just as how your arms and back can, except your mind works mentally rather than physically.

What do you think would happen if you did not exercise your brain? If you think nothing would change, that is where you are wrong. Many people have the misconception that their brain will function the same forever, and that is why dementia and Alzheimer's are so devastating and tragic in our eyes. You see it as an unavoidable tragedy, but the truth is, they can be avoided if you treat your mind like a muscle. Work it out, and feed it the right nutrition.

Think of your day as a workout for your brain. Do you go to the gym every day and just focus on your chest? No. You most likely rotate your exercises in a pattern so that every part of your body gets a workout. You should do the same with your mind. Find different exercises for your brain and cycle through them.

Just as how you can hit a wall with a workout, so you can with your concentration. When hitting this wall, you simply have to dig a deeper to sought the motivation that will push through. A promise of reward can help. Nevertheless, working hard will strengthen your brain – your memory. Here are some useful tips that will definitely help you do just that:

Fighting for Attention

Technology can both save and destroy our attention spans. While there are apps you can use that silence your phone during times where you need to focus, a lot of people do not have the will power to do so with vigor. Many people will find themselves turning off this app and going back to using their phones and being distracted.

Humans are easily distracted creatures. That is why robots are so popular. They can do twice the work most humans can because they do not get distracted. As a whole, the human race could seriously use some work on their attention skills.

Of course, if you are reading this, you probably want to improve all of your cognitive skills. Whether it may be to combat the robots, or just to get through the work day, it is good that you want to fight the technology blues and get back to a strong mind.

One of the easiest ways to get a strong attention span is to go zen. Zen is where you get so lost in your work that you forget the world around you even exists. This is a wonderful thing because when you are in that state, you forget your troubles and your worries. It may seem a little strange that you want to get lost in your work that much, but it can make the time go faster, and you can learn so much more because at that moment it is just you and your information.

Meditation is a great way to help yourself achieve a zen state of mind. Meditation involves getting out of your body and into your mind. You do not have to sit cross legged and mutter "hmmm, " but you do have to be comfortable enough to let your body move over so you can enter your own brain.

When you meditate, you will have a moment where it seems like everything on your body itches. You will have the urge to scratch everywhere. Your body likes to be the center of attention. Ignore it, and it will grudgingly allow your mind to take over. Once you are in this state, you can focus more clearly on your work. From there you will find the clarity of mind that you have is out of this world, and you will learn so much more.

Everyone faces the struggle of maintaining focus. That is normal and is something that you should not be ashamed of. However, if it regularly causes you delay with your work, then you should probably strive to become better at focusing. This chapter contains a bunch of tips that will help you do so. These tips are even more perfect for people who struggle with attention deficiency.

Everyone struggles from time to time when it comes to maintaining focus. That is nothing to be ashamed of. However, if it regularly impedes with your work, then you should strive to become better at focusing. This entire chapter is filled with tips on how to do so, and here are even more. These tips are for people who struggle with attention deficiency.

PART 2

Chapter 1: Health Benefits of Decluttering

The idea of clutter has many different

meanings. In its simplest terms, it explains the physical things that provide no real meaning, but just fill space. These things can be anything from a pile of old newspapers in your home, to clothes that no longer fit, or something that just no longer serves a purpose. While these physical objects are truly just "things" that take up space in your home, they also take up space in your mind.

Right now, you are likely sitting at home or at work reading this book. Take a look around. Is your space clean and clutter-free, or are there a bunch of little things all around you? More importantly, do all of those little things actually serve a purpose, or are you not really sure why they are there?

If you aren't sure why you have so many

things, it is time to seriously consider decluttering your space. You see, stuff isn't just stuff, it develops an emotional connection within you. A cluttered home indicates a cluttered mind, and a cluttered home also causes a disorganized mind. This is a two-way street. The clutter probably built up because of distraction within your brain.

Many of us don't feel the need to save a pile of junk mail, yet there it may sit on the kitchen counter for weeks. A clear, undistracted mind would have the capability to quickly and systematically sort through that mail, and discard the unimportant things. Instead, the mind thinks of ten other things at once, and going through the mail becomes a daunting task. When you feel distracted, it is easy to let the little things go, which leads to unneeded things cluttering your life.

Unfortunately, this is a vicious circle. Yes, your mind was working on ten different projects before the mail came, but by not getting through the mail pile, you have inadvertently created the eleventh, furthering your mind from being free. The "stuff" is both the cause and effect of a cluttered mind, and the only way to break that cycle is to decrease the clutter.

Not only are those excess things causing a cluttered mind, they also hold emotional baggage. Think about that pair of jeans sitting in your closet. They were a size too small when you bought them, but at that time, you promised yourself that you would lose a few pounds and they would fit. Several years later, they still sit there, in the bag you brought them home in, with the tags still on. They are no longer just a pair of pants, they are a sign of failure. You failed to reach your weight loss goal, and those pants are a daily reminder of your shortcomings. Getting dressed in the morning should not come with a dose of negativity.

Any type of object could hold negative thoughts and feelings, and we must recognize these things and remove them from our lives. The simple act of removing something that evokes bad feelings or memories can have a tremendous effect on our mental health and emotional state. Decluttering can be a very emotional process for some due to these connections. For example, after losing a loved one, it is common for mourners to keep rooms or other living spaces exactly as the deceased left it. The things inside that room become a sort of shrine to the departed, and instead of being inanimate objects, become an emotional crutch. For some, it may be necessary to seek help from a therapist to deal with the emotional connection before getting rid of the things.

From an artistic standpoint, a mess of clutter is unappealing to the eye. In art, it is the artists' responsibility to draw the eye in at a focal point, and let the eye flow over the picture and back to the focal point in a swift, easy motion. When someone doesn't know where to look, the brain gets confused and begins to use more energy searching for a focal point. The same is true with the spaces we inhabit. If your bedroom has clothes all over the floor, and the bedsheets and blankets crumpled into a ball, your eyes see chaos and expend more energy trying to make sense of it. You are draining your own emotional energy by living in this environment. When was the last time you saw a cluttered room on the front page of a home improvement magazine?

Decluttering gives your mind more time to focus on important things. By removing menial thoughts of cleaning up the house, it leaves more room for focusing on tasks at work, or simply becoming more present in your life. Many people find that decluttering actually enhances their performance at work. As their brains become less distracted, they have more power to focus on projects at work, and their energy and mental focus are greatly improved.

This can translate to other areas of life, like being mentally present when hanging out with friends, spouses, and kids, leading to more meaningful and satisfying relationships. Studies prove that having these types of relationships in your life is a direct indicator of happiness and improved mental status.

Many professional organizers can attest to improvements of their clients' mental as well as physical health. The immediate decrease in stress by changing the living environment boosts the mood and energy, lowers blood pressure and promotes health and weight loss, likely due from overall decreases in stress. In extreme cases, like hoarding, excess clutter gathers dust and critters that live in the mess. This could be a health hazard, creating breathing problems and increases the risk of fire.

Take another look around. What is the

current state of your surroundings? If you are feeling overwhelmed by the chaos of clutter around you, or even think that some minor improvements can be made, go ahead and get started. Make a commitment to reduce your clutter for the sake of your physical health and well-being.

Chapter 2: Joys Of Simple Living

Over the past decade or so, our culture has taken a drastic turn. Earlier decades played up the need for having extravagant things. Buying new cars, the best new video games, and fancy new clothes every season was the norm, and if you wanted to have any sort of popular status, this is what you did.

Besides the problems in funding behind these habits, we found that having all of this "stuff" really served no emotional purpose. Things don't make you truly happy, and buying a new pair of shoes every time things get tough causes you to avoid solving the problem. As this fact came to light, many people started to shy away from physical things and were drawn more to meaningful relationships and memorable experiences as a way to find happiness in life. While there are still many stragglers on this earth, studies have shown that people who have less "stuff" are generally happier in life. So, there is only one reasonable conclusion; get rid of your clutter!

The things in your home should only be those that bring you joy or serve a regular purpose. Hanging on to other things that you may use someday, like those jeans that are two sizes too small, really serves no purpose. It is time to retrain your brain to look at your things as the inanimate objects that they are. Things only have meaning because we cause them to. The baseball you brought home from a game isn't special, it is the memory of going to that game with your family. Hold on to the memory (and a few pictures), but remember that the baseball is just a baseball.

Take it one step further. That baseball could be used to create more great memories. If you or your kids aren't interested in playing with it, give it to the kids down the block. Take note when you see them outside playing, knowing that you brought them a little bit of joy. That is worth much more than leather and string.

Most importantly, get rid of things that trigger bad memories. This can be a tough thing, especially if you feel that keeping certain items are a replacement for something you have lost. Unfortunately, we all lost people, or favorite pets over the course of our lives. Let's say your dog died, and you decide to hold on to their collar. That collar may bring back memories of great times with your dog, but may also make you sad that they're gone. While it's okay to miss them, that collar is not required to have those memories. If you were to take a souvenir from every memory you ever had, your house would be filled to the brim.

If you feel ready, donate the collar to another

dog. Whether that means adopting a new dog or giving it to a friend, give that collar good use and honor your fallen friend by letting her live on. If you're not ready to take that step, go ahead and keep it. That's right, keep it. Having certain things of meaning in your home is important as well. But maybe get rid of the old dog toys as a compromise. Once you are ready to let go, make that choice.

Simple living isn't just limited to the physical things in life, it is also the processes in which we live our daily life. The majority of people would say they hit the ground running as soon as the alarm goes off. They are pulled in different directions, trying to pack lunches and get kids on the bus, satisfying the needs of others at work, then going to obligatory meetings like PTA, or community council meetings. Remember that events in your calendar are "things" too. They are things that are getting in the way of your happiness. If you truly enjoy these things, go ahead and keep them in your schedule. If you hate extracurricular meetings after work, take a step back.

Life is meant to be lived in a satisfying way. If you feel that your current course of activities is simply to please others, it is time to reevaluate your priorities. Make happiness a priority too. There will be things you have to do, but you don't have to do those things all the time. Start scheduling in fun activities instead of doing them only when there is extra time.

Take a look at your calendar. Change the color of all work events to blue, or a color of choice. Next, make obligatory meetings, like book club, yellow. Finally, make fun outings pink. What does your calendar look like? Is it a sea of blue and yellow, or a colorful patchwork of work and fun?

As you plan next week, mark out some time for doing a workout class with a friend, catching up on reading, or any other activity that brings you joy. While we all have obligations, a life isn't worth living if that work isn't balanced out by a bit of fun. Learn how to say 'no' if a special project just doesn't seem appealing, and set some time aside for things you truly love. You won't want to get to the end of your life and realize you just worked.

Chapter 3: Clutter Overhaul

Now that you realize how important decluttering can be to your overall health, it's time to make a plan. How you will carry out that plan will really depend on the level of clutter in your home. For the sake of covering everyone, let's say you have developed quite a bit of clutter, in which only about half of the things in your home have any use to you. This might be you if every stable surface in your home is loaded with things, you constantly trip over stuff, or if you have entire rooms you have not entered in years, due to a number of things that have accumulated.

While it may seem overwhelming, the best thing to do is rip off the bandage and just get started. Clear your schedule for an entire weekend, or plan to take a couple of days off from work, to spend cleaning and organizing. Set up a schedule for yourself if that makes it seem a little less overwhelming. While there is something to be said for making changes a little bit at a time, sometimes it's easier to get these things done in one big session, rather than dragging out the process. If you feel that a big cleanout is not feasible, do what you can, and at least commit to a daily 5 minute declutter, which will be discussed in the last chapter.

Start with the most frequently used room in the house. Dedicate your time to completing this one room before moving on. Look at it and make a mental checklist of the things that need to be done, then go ahead and tackle it.

Before you begin, make sure you have a plan to get rid of these things. Simply moving them to other rooms, or bagging it all up to sit on the porch, have a clear plan for things to move to other locations besides your home. This can mean a few things. You can either bite the bullet and throw things away, like true garbage, sell items of value, like collectibles you no longer care about or donate gently used items to others. While it is best to recycle what you can, sometimes figuring out the minute details of getting that done can be overwhelming. Try to figure it out ahead of time so you don't get discouraged while you clean.

Call up a local shelter or charity to let them know you have children's toys, or old clothing, or anything else that might be helpful. This serves as a place to dispense of old items, and getting others involved makes you committed to your cleanout. This is especially important if you either do have things of great value, like collectibles you no longer want, or useful things that you will have a hard time throwing in the trash.

Take regular breaks, drinking water and eating, to keep up your strength and willpower. One of the reasons we avoid overhauls like this is because it is mentally and physically draining. It can be emotionally equivalent to packing all of your things and moving. Just exhausting. Take breaks, revisit why you are doing this to begin with, and keep up the motivation.

If you have a hard time letting things go, develop a system to get through it. For example, if you feel that everything is sentimental, like the same level as the dog collar, a simple set of rules can help you distinguish between truly sentimental and borderline hoarding tendencies.

Rules for decluttering:

Rule #1: If you haven't used an item in over 6 months, it's time to let go.

Rule #2: If you didn't know you had an item, and it serves no purpose to better your life, let it go.

Rule #3: If an item brings back negative memories or emotions, let go.

Don't be afraid to ask for help. Just like moving, decluttering may be something your friends or family will dread helping with. But, as friends and family do, they can recognize a plea for help and would like to help you improve your life. Ask for a bit of help, and make sure to keep the mood light and airy as you work. Commiserating about all of the things still left to do will only bring the process down. Decluttering is about freeing yourself, so keep the tone that way.

Certain cases of clutter require a bit more help and don't be afraid to ask. Some of you reading this may have a legitimate problem with hoarding. There has been a lot of light shed on this problem in recent years, as TV programs have been dedicated to this subject. While the people on those shows are fascinating cases, the underlying psychological issues that are associated with this habit are apparent.

Just like a substance abuse or overeating problem, hoarding tendencies are a real, diagnosable problem that can be treated with therapy and with the help of a professional organizer. To generalize, people who hoard either never learned proper housekeeping habits, or use their hoarding as a coping mechanism for past or current trauma, like the death of a loved one, or abuse, much like someone with a drug problem would. It is important not to make light of people who have this type of problem. Hoarding is an addiction too.

Good did come from the spotlight, however. Therapy services and professional organizing and cleanup services specialize in managing hoards, and the media showed how the recovery process worked so that people with no idea where to start fixing their problem had a guide to help them. There is nothing worse than recognizing you have a problem, but not knowing how to fix it. Seek the help of a therapist if you feel there are underlying issues attached to your collecting and saving tendencies. At least, they will help you get to the root of the problem to stop the habit, but they also will likely have ideas to help you clean up, giving references to local companies. Seeking out help will probably be the most difficult, but most beneficial step in the healing process.

No matter your level of decluttering, use these rules to help get started. As you make decisions to get rid of things, your mind will start to clear and you will have the confidence to complete your project and better your life. If you begin to feel overwhelmed, think about how nice your home will look, and how clear your thoughts will be when you're done!

Chapter 4: The 5 Minute Daily Declutter

Five minutes isn't long. It takes about five minutes to brew a pot of coffee, go outside and get the mail, or even brush your teeth. Why not devote just five minutes a day to decluttering your home, for the sake of your health?

If you completed an entire decluttering overhaul, as outlined in Chapter 3, a five minute declutter should be just about all you need to maintain your clutter-free home. After all, once you start from scratch, you should no longer have piles of things to put away, just what is left over from the day.

The time of day in which you complete this five minutes is up to you, but many people benefit from doing this as part of their morning routine. If you leave it for the end of the day, you will likely be tired and mentally drained. Purposefully picking things up and putting them where they belong can sometimes take a bit of thought, which you will likely have more energy for first thing in the morning.

So today, after you finish reading this book, set a timer for five minutes. Use the timer on your phone or microwave. Begin picking up things that don't belong where they are, like clothes on the floor, junk mail sitting on the counter, anything that is out of place. Likely, you will find yourself getting impatient with your own daily habits. In five minutes a day, you will begin to realize just how much chaos you accumulate in one day. Why couldn't you have put the clothes in the laundry basket across the room once you took them off? Why did you wait until the next day to put them in there?

As you begin to notice these annoying self-habits, you will likely correct them, leading to less clutter in the first place. Your five minutes will become more and more productive, as less time will be needed for the things you should have done, to begin with.

It is important to do one item at a time during your five minutes. Pick up the clothes and either fold and put them away, or throw them in the laundry basket. Put the book you finished back on the shelf, instead of letting it sit on the coffee table. Purposefully put each item where it belongs, don't just stick it on an already-overflowing shelf. No, you won't go back to it later, do it now.

Make a point to start in a different room

each day. Constantly starting in the kitchen, then living room, then bedroom, means that the dining room never gets any attention. Each day, start in the room that needs the most attention or has had the most neglect.

If you didn't participate in a full home overhaul, your space may need a bit more work. Let's say your kitchen needs to be reorganized. Use that daily five minutes to clean out one drawer at a time, moving or getting rid of things that don't belong in that drawer, or things you simply have no use for. While it will take a lot longer to completely declutter your home with five minutes a day, if decluttering is emotionally draining for you, five minutes may be all you can handle. When you're feeling motivated, go ahead and do more, but commit yourself to at least five minutes. It will be over before you know it!

Chapter 5: Organization 101

The primary purpose for decluttering your living space is for functionality, and that starts with organization. Think about the layout of your kitchen. If you wanted to make a batch of brownies right now, can you think of where all of the ingredients are? The pan to cook it in? Like many of us, that baking pan is probably at the bottom of a stack of pans and involves a bit of finagling to get it out of its hiding place. Perhaps you don't know where your baking chocolate or flour is. The goal of the organization is for everything important to have its place so that you know where to find it. In the grand scheme of things, this will save you time, and an exorbitant amount of frustration when it comes to daily tasks.

Take this mindset to other areas of your home. Is all of your makeup stuffed in a single bag? And where is that red lipstick? These little, seemingly insignificant thoughts, on top of a hundred others, can leave you mentally drained before you even leave the house in the morning. Just thinking of it now may make you feel a bit overwhelmed. If everything had a place, and you knew where to look, everyday tasks would become just a bit easier, leaving energy for your mind to focus on more pertinent things.

Now is the time to take action. Now that you have gotten rid of a lot of things that you simply don't need, it is time to organize your daily essentials in a way that fits your needs. All of the things you need to get ready for work in the morning should be in the same place. Your clothes should be clean, folded or hung, and ready to go. Your toothpaste, deodorant, and other hygiene products should be in one place. In the kitchen, your egg pan should be clean and put away, ready for use, and as you pack your lunch, you shouldn't be digging in the back of the cabinet to find a lid for the plastic wear. All of these things add up to wasted valuable time.

Decide to organize one room at a time. It is important to focus on one space. Take the kitchen, for example. Take a few minutes to think about your normal kitchen workflow. If you are constantly searching for a spatula or wooden spoon while you cook, make sure to store those utensils in a drawer closest to the stove. Knives and cutting boards should be relatively close to each other. Baking pans should have racks. Utilize counter space only for those things you use every single day, like a blender or toaster. If you are short on counter space, keep your work area as clutter-free as possible to avoid frustration. Everything should have a place, and you shouldn't have to move five things to do one simple task.

Next, systematically go through your closets. We all have that one closet that becomes a dumping ground. Kids closets are often filled with broken or unused toys. Likely, the things they like most are out in their bedroom, so the closet is a great place to start when thinning the junk. First, get rid of anything broken. Don't fall for the practical side of your brain when it says, "I can fix that!". If you do not actively fix that within a few minutes, it will just continue to sit in the closet. Get rid of it!

Clothes in an adult closet are the same as toys. If there are clothes you never wear, that don't fit, or simply aren't your style, why do you have them? Since clothes are expensive, it can be hard to let go. Do your best to give away clothes that are still in good shape. Give things to friends, sell them at a consignment shop, or donate them to charity. For old clothes with holes and stains, throw them out, or throw them in the rag pile in the garage. They will still be good for dusting the house or checking the oil in your car. Just don't get carried away. Save a few good ones and discard the rest.

No home is complete without a junk drawer. This is a place where all of the little things that just don't fit in go. Store things like batteries, tape, thumbtacks, glue and other small items in your junk drawer. You may think this isn't organized, but it truly is.

Everything has its place, and if it doesn't it's placed is the junk drawer. In the event you need one of these random items, you will know exactly where to look. Over time, your junk drawer will upgrade to a magic junk drawer, producing just the right item when you need it most!

When it comes to organization and decluttering, it is best to use what you already have, and avoid buying more things to keep in your home. Use old baskets or bags for storage. Reorganize dressers and bureaus to fit more, and utilize space under the bed.

In some cases, it will be necessary to buy organizational products. A full closet organizer system probably isn't required for most people, but a pack of new hangers and a couple of baskets can turn a closet into a more organized, functional space. Purchase large, flat containers to store off-season clothes under the bed, or a filing cabinet to keep your important papers organized. Just don't go overboard, as you will end up with more junk! Think function.

PART 3

1

Chapter 1: Different Emotions and How to Handle Them

There are many different emotions that a person experiences and each one of these emotions can have a range of facets that make what each person feels a wholly unique experience. This means that what you experience when you meet a new person will be entirely different from the experience you would get from anyone else. Every person is a different feeling when you first meet them, and this is a great way to learn to distinguish whose feelings you are feeling, even when you cannot experience them.

However, to be able to distinguish a person from the emotional identification card they leave, you must first be able to first understand the different emotions and be able to distinguish them from the other emotions in the atmosphere. You also have to learn how to harness them for yourself, and really get in tune with them Then, eventually, you will be able to identify someone by the emotions they leave behind. This chapter will inform you of the different emotions, and how you can understand them better.

Happiness

Happiness is a common emotion for people to experience, however, it has many different factors in it. There are several layers of happiness, and you have to be able to discern each one from the next. Being able to do this is one of the most difficult things an emotional master does because happiness is one of the most complex emotion a person feels.

Think of the best thing in your life. How it made you feel. Now think of the day you got some good news. The happiness you experienced in those two events was probably exponentially different. This is how happiness works. You can be mildly happy, or you can be happy while sad at the same time, or you can be extremely happy. There are so many different types of happiness that it can make your head spin.

For this book, we will focus on the main types of happiness, so as not to cause information overload. Here are the main types of happiness.

Joy

This is the emotion that many people experience when they hear good news. It is the emotion you experience when you find out someone you know is going to have a baby. It is the basis for all happy moments. Joy is the emotion you feel when you wake up on a Saturday morning and realize that you do not have to go to work that day, and can sleep in an extra hour. Joy is the emotion you feel when you find out that you have a little more money in the bank than you originally thought.

This is the most common happiness that people feel. It can be strong, or it can be mild. It can hit all at once, or it can build gradually. Joy is everywhere around you. People often mistake joy for other emotions of happiness, however, believing that they are synonymous. They might be in the English

language, but they are not synonymous in the
emotional IQ culture. Each emotion is separate, not
all considered one. Joy is the basic emotion of
happiness, but it is not the only one.

Elation

Elation is another facet of the emotion of happiness.
Elation is what you experience when you find out
you got the job promotion that you have been
wanting for so long. Elation is the emotion that
people who have been waiting years to conceive
experience when they find out that they are
expecting a baby. Elation is the purest level of
happiness. It leaves the person experiencing it
feeling like they are on cloud nine, and like they
have never felt anything better. This is the emotion
of happiness that everyone seeks out and wants to
experience on a regular basis.

Most people experience elation the best when they
have been through a period of sadness. The sadness
allows them to truly appreciate the happiness that

has been bestowed upon them. When people feel truly elated, it is because something that they have wanted to happen for a long time finally happened after a long period of struggling.

Excitement

Most people know what excitement is. It is the emotion you experience when you are wanting something, and you know that it is coming, and you are so happy that you cannot wait for it to be here. Like a kid on Christmas, or an expectant mother, to someone waiting for a package in the mail. You cannot beat the feeling of excitement. It is the most contagious of emotions that are out there. When someone sees that another person is excited, they get excited for them, just so they can feel excited too.

Most people want to feel excited about each day as they wake up, however, this is nearly impossible to achieve. They can, however, achieve the next emotion of happiness that is on our list.

General Contentment

This is the last emotion of happiness that is on the list. This is what most people strive for in their life. While most people want to experience excitement every day, they are generally willing to settle for general contentment. That is because general contentment is a great feeling to have. It is when you wake up every day thinking that it is going to be a good day, and you are generally pleased with the day's occurrences. People who experience general contentment are happier people, and they are the ones you see who think that life is great.

There are a lot of people that try to fake general contentment when in reality they are not happy at all. However, since you are reading this book, you can probably already spot those people from a mile away. The people with true general contentment are the ones that you can feel the calm rolling off of them. They are the roll with the punches kind of people that you see that never have a bad thing to say about the day no matter what day you see them. Even on Mondays.

Those are the main facets of the emotion happiness. There are more subtle ones, but you could write an entire book on all the subtle nuances of happiness, and for a beginner, that is a lot of information to process in one sitting. These ones are the ones that you will experience most in the beginning. However, there are many places that you can research online to learn more about this emotion when you are ready.

Sadness

Sadness is an emotion a lot of people face. It is pretty complex as well, just like with happiness. However, it does not have as many facets, just different levels of sadness. These levels do not really have names, and they are hard to identify as anything other than sadness. The difference is when someone is depressed, as opposed to sad. With depression, not only is the sadness overwhelming, the complete apathy for everything that rolls off of them is scary. Yet, when you look at the faces of these people, they seem like the happiest people on earth.

Sadness is not depression, though. Sadness is just an emotion that you experience when something that is upsetting happens. You can experience sadness when you do not get something right, or do not get what you want. These are a few of the more general types of sadness. The slightly dark feeling you get when you are upset.

Sadness can also raise in intensity. The feeling of sadness you get after a bad break up, for example. The cliché is that the woman sits on her couch watching chick flicks while eating ice cream straight from the tub, and the guy goes out to the bar to drink away the pain. However, many people cope with sadness differently. Some may stay in bed until they feel better, some may go for a run to make themselves feel better.

Sadness can increase in intensity even more than the pain you feel during a breakup. The sadness you feel when tragedy strikes. Such as losing a loved one or a pet. This sadness can easily turn into depression if not addressed soon enough. This level of sadness often feels like a hole has been ripped in your chest. Like you could never breathe again. This is the worst type of sadness, and the hardest to get through, but if someone can get through it, they may be able to escape the grasp of depression.

Anger

Anger is one of the least complex emotions you will experience. It is pretty straightforward. However, it is also the hardest emotion to describe. Anger is like a searing branding iron is trying to rip its way out of your soul through your stomach. It leaves you feeling like you want to scream, or punch someone, or curse up a storm. I think the reason that anger is so hard to explain is that everyone experienced it so differently. It may not be very complex in that it doesn't have a lot of levels or facets, but it is experienced differently by person to person. More so than any other emotion out there. Anger can cause a wash of sadness over some people. Some people when they are angry feel strangely happy. Some people respond with mild anger on intense things, but rage on little things. It is all dependent on the person themselves, and that is why anger can be one of the hardest things to explain.

Anger can be found in many places. Most of the time it is when someone is mean to another person, however, some people respond to sad things with anger. Anger is often used as a synonym for frustration, but this is not the case. Far from it, actually. Frustration is just mild irritation at a slight annoyance. Anger is the feeling of great agitation at things that are considered harmful or offensive.

Jealousy

This is an emotion that everyone will experience in their lifetime, but no one will want to admit it. That is because, in a lot of religions, it is considered a sin. This one is one of the most hidden emotions, but one of the easiest to feel once you are tuned into it. Jealousy is the emotion that people experience when they want something that someone else has. Jealousy is also used to describe how a woman or man feels in a relationship. Do not confuse this, as it is not truly jealousy. Jealousy is when you want something that is not yours. When you already have something, and you want to protect it, that is being territorial.

Jealousy is often felt with a sick feeling in the stomach and is portrayed as a puke green aura. Have you ever heard the phrases "green with envy" or "sick with jealousy"? These are because that is the energy that this emotion gives off, and can really affect an emotional master because it is a strong emotion, due to the fact that it is generally buried deep beneath the surface, and it builds pressure until it is to the point where if it were a gas, it would cause the person feeling this emotion to literally explode.

Those are the different emotions that people experience on a regular, or semi-regular basis. Now that you know them, and their basic identifiers, you can move on to how to harness their usage to handle a situation.

Chapter 2: Meditation for Emotion

There are many ways to unlock your emotional IQ and really access it, but meditation is the best way to do so. It allows you to center yourself enough to make sure that you are finding the right part of yourself to unlock. A lot of times even if you do not do it right, you can trick yourself into thinking that you have, and you will feel like you are seeing the world when really it is a placebo effect and you are just as blind as you were before. So meditation is a great choice, though other choices will be discussed in a later chapter just to cover all options.

What is Meditation?

Meditation is the act of calming yourself and slowing your breathing to truly find your center. It is used by people from all walks of life, though it is mainly attributed to being used by monks to find inner peace. However, anyone can meditate and find it effective. You do not have to be an expert either. There are so many tutorials out there. This chapter will cover meditation techniques as well, to ensure that you are learning everything you need to know about opening your emotional IQ. You want to open it to find yourself, and meditation will help with that.

Meditation involves being able to sit still for long periods of time, so it can be difficult at first. Even more so if you are someone who is always moving, and never slows down. Because you have to slow down for meditation to even work. When you are meditating, you are literally putting yourself into a trance, and your heart will slow to the pace that it functions at when you are asleep.

Meditation is used to find spirituality, along with a whole list of other things, including the emotional IQ. Here is a list of things that meditation helps with.

- 🏭 Anxiety: Anxiety is a problem that plagues a lot of people. It causes raised heart rate, intense and sometimes borderline asthmatic breathing problems, and thoughts that can be suicidal, or homicidal. Anxiety attacks can leave the person who suffers from them emotionally and physically exhausted. Anxiety is also something that can be almost entirely cured my meditation
🏭

The reason for that is when you meditate you calm yourself enough to figure out what is causing your anxiety so you can address and fix the problem. You want to be able to do that when it comes to your inner eye so that your vision is not clouded by your fears and panic attacks.

- Stress: Stress can cause a lot of problems in your life. It is the number one cause of heart attacks due to the fact that it can raise your blood pressure. It can also cause strokes and other health issues. You do not want to die due to stress as it is not a pleasant way to go.

Meditation helps you slow your heart rate and work through the things that are bothering you to ensure that you are living a healthy lifestyle. You want to be healthy, otherwise, you will find that your life will not be as enjoyable as you would hope. You want to enjoy your life. Stress can also cloud your emotional IQ just as anxiety does, and it can cause anxiety as well. You want to have a freed up emotional IQ so that you can find yourself.

- Ease Pain: By slowing your heart and breath rate, you are dulling the nerve endings in your body, allowing the pain receptors to have a break. This helps you recover from severe pain, and end chronic pain. Pain can affect your everyday life in ways that some people can never imagine. It leaves you tired, drained, and wondering where you are going to get the energy to even eat.

You do not want to live with chronic pain, but unfortunately, some people have no choice. If you meditate, however, you will be able to ease your pain for a while in order to get your energy back so that you can take on the world. This is a good thing because pain can cloud your mind, not just your emotional IQ, but your entire mind.

- Calm Your Soul: This is a good thing that you can use meditation for. If anything is bothering you, you can use meditation to really figure out what exactly is nagging at the back of your mind. You want to have a clear head when you go to use your emotional IQ, otherwise, you will find that what is bothering you will make its way into your sight and cause you to have some issues deciphering what is real and what is fabricated by your emotions.

It is important to separate your emotions from your emotional IQ because you have to stay completely neutral on any topic you are looking for clarity on. Otherwise, your "vision" may be skewed in the direction of your worry. You do not want that to happen, as it can cause unnecessary stress, which as mentioned above is bad for your health.

📅 Stabilize Your Life: It is important to stabilize your life because maintaining balance is essential to succeed in your life. If you do not have balance, you will have problems keeping an organized life. Having a clear and stable life is good for your health as well because you are more likely to make healthier choices. This will extend your life and make it easier to access your emotional IQ. It is proven that the healthier you are, the easier it is to clear your mind.

There are many other things that meditation can do for some people that it cannot do for others. It is best to try it for yourself to see if it works for you. Of course, if you do not know how to meditate, it can make it harder to do so, so let us go over how to meditate successfully.

How to Meditate

There are many different ways to meditate, but meditation is important to do correctly, otherwise, you will find yourself not getting the full benefits of the process, as you would if you do it correctly. So for a beginner, it is best to not take any shortcuts and to really go the full nine yards to do it correctly.

It will take some time to really learn how to clear your mind, so if you do not get it on the first try, do not get discouraged. No one gets it on the first try, and that can get frustrating, but it is completely normal. You want to keep trying to clear your mind. If you get discouraged after the first try, you won't be able to truly know if you can do it or not. Media portrays meditation as something you can do with ease and something that everyone is able to just sit and do, but it is not. It takes a lot of self-restraint. So let's go over the steps.

- Step One: The first step is to find a quiet place where you will not be interrupted. Even if it means going into the bathroom and turning the shower on to find some peace and quiet. You have to be quiet and undisturbed in order to find your inner peace. If you are not in a peaceful area, finding your center will be extremely hard because there will be so many distractions in the area that you will not be able to concentrate on yourself.

Step Two: Sit in a comfortable position. A lot of people choose the crossed leg style because that is what they know, but if it is not a comfortable position for you, then you will not be able to focus on yourself because you will be too distracted by your leg going numb, your back hurting, your hips getting stiff. If you cannot focus on anything other than your discomfort, then you are not going to be able to successfully meditate. So find the most comfortable sitting position for you, even if it means in a chair. However, do not lay down. It is too easy to fall asleep if you are laying down, because your body equates the slow heartbeat and breathing with sleep, and your brain will begin to slow as well. You want the health benefits of sleeping with the full mental capabilities of being awake. Otherwise, you will not be able to probe your mind the way you would when sitting. How you sit does not matter, as long as you are comfortable.

- Step Three: Focus on your breathing. Most people say to focus on your heart rate at first, but that is a lot harder, and if you slow your breathing, generally your heart will follow suit. You want to really focus on your breath though. Do not let yourself get distracted. Breathe in for four counts and out for four counts. Balance is key. In fact, why don't you give it a try right now? You don't have to try to meditate, just work on the breathing.

Sit comfortably, and close your eyes. Breathe in for four counts through your nose. Hold it for two counts, and then let it out of your mouth for four seconds. Focus on keeping a steady rhythm. If you lose count, then start again. You have to make sure that you are keeping the rhythm and not losing count, otherwise, you will not be able to focus on the meditation if you can't keep your breathing steady. Try doing a repetition of ten, and once you get that down, try upping it to twenty, and so on and so forth. The longer you can go while focusing on your breathing, the easier it will be to transition your focus to your mental state once you get to that point.

- Step Four: Ignore the twinges. This is something that is one of the hardest things to do when you are trying to get into meditation because our bodies are not meant to sit still for extended periods of time. After five to ten minutes of sitting still, you will begin to feel itchy in places such as your nose or your head. Maybe your leg will start to feel like it is going to fall asleep. Ignore all of these. They are signals from your brain to your body checking to see if you are asleep yet or not. Once the brain realizes that the body is not responding, then it will command the body to shut down all processes as if you were asleep. If you are still awake, you will get all of the benefits of being asleep, while still getting to enjoy the benefits of being awake in a calm, unfazed perception.

- Step Five: Once you get into this phase of pretty much lucid dreaming, slowly transition your focus from your breathing to your mind. Do this by only focusing on every other count and when you are not focusing on your count, then focus on a thought that has been on your mind all day. Eventually, you can switch your focus entirely to that thought. Once you are ready to move on you can think of other thoughts slowly until you are fully immersed in your own mind.

- Step Six: Explore your mind freely. Get to know every little nook and cranny of your brain. This step will take some time to get to, as you will need to be able to hold the meditation stage for quite a while before you can freely explore your mind. However, once you get to this stage, you will be able to learn more about yourself than you probably ever wanted to know. This is important because you want to know everything about yourself. This includes the good, bad, and even the ugly. The more you know, the more clear your vision can be.

Step Seven: This is the final step of meditation, known as the outro. A lot of people think that you can just snap out of a meditation, and some people can, although it is not very healthy for you because the sudden return of a normal heart rate stresses your heart out, and it can cause some severe headaches as well. You have to gradually enter yourself back into reality. If you do not, you will have a problem with being confused, headaches, and much more. To come back to reality without these problems, simply revert your focus slowly back onto your breathing, and focus on speeding up your breathing until your heart rate returns to normal.

Once you have successfully managed to meditate for the first time, you will find that every time after that you can begin to get a little faster with your meditation. This is a good thing because when you meditate, sometimes you do not have a lot of time, however, you still have to ease out of it. So it is good to be able to get quick at it in order to have ample time to ease out of it.

Remember, the first several times it can be extremely difficult for you to get into a trance state if you even manage to at all. Do not get discouraged if you cannot do it immediately. Also, even if you do get into a trance state it may be hard for you to maintain it for any length of time. This is normal and is nothing to feel bad about. Keep trying, and eventually, you will be able to meditate like a Tibetan Monk.

2

Chapter 3: Self-Discipline

It is important for you to have self-discipline when you want to improve your emotional IQ. It will help you harness your emotions exponentially so that you can work on keeping them under control. Here is how you can do that.

About Improving Self Discipline

You are probably aware that self-discipline is a great trait to have, and maybe you are not as disciplined as you should be. If that is the case, you may find it hard to keep your mind and emotions in check. If you are not able to control your emotions, your emotional IQ will be way below what it should be.

To truly understand self-discipline, you must first know the definition of what it is.

Self-discipline is defined as the ability to find a reason to stick with something for a long period of time, even if you may not want to. Especially if you do not want to.

This may seem confusing because it doesn't seem possible to find a reason to do something when you obviously do not want to do it. However, the truth is that there are reasons you may never have even known about to do what you do not want to do. Most of those come from inside yourself. The biggest reason should be for your emotional health. The more it wears down, the less you understand your own emotions.

Why You Should Improve

Do you have days where you just feel worn out? Maybe not even just physically, but mentally and emotionally as well? Do those days seem to be more often than not? If this is the case, you need to work on handling your emotions with more strength and understanding.

The reason you feel so drained is that you are letting yourself get too emotionally worked up by little things. It is human nature to get upset easily it seems. However, with a little effort in the discipline area, you can increase your emotional strength and intelligence quite a bit. This will help you find the strength to ignore the irritating things and live a happier life.

1 What it Takes to Develop Self-Discipline

No one is born with innate amounts of self-discipline. We are all born with a need to take care of, rather than a need to take care of others. That is why babies are not born able to walk. You have to develop yourself discipline beyond what you may naturally develop growing up.

Most people need a few things to happen to be able to work on their self-discipline, and that is okay because developing self-discipline in itself takes a form of discipline that not everyone is used to.

You have to know how to build your self-discipline though, as it does not happen overnight. You should also remember that you have taken years to be who you are, and you should not expect to change completely in a short amount of time. You have to give yourself the time to really become a better, more disciplined person. One of the hardest things about having self-discipline is developing it, and a lot of people give up before they hit their goal. So always remember to never give up, and to follow these tips to help you out.

1 Keeping Yourself Accountable

You are responsible for your own emotions. You cannot hold someone else responsible for how you feel, even if they make you feel that way. You can ask them to apologize for upsetting you, but in the end, it is up to you to feel better. Wallowing in your self-pity, and holding a grudge shows a low emotional IQ, and is what you want to work to stay away from. At the end of the day, you should be able to let go of everything that is bothering you and set yourself free from the chains of negativity.

2 Having Rewards and Penalties

Just like when you were a child, you should reward yourself for the good, and penalize yourself for the bad. Remember, you have to hold yourself accountable, and this means to only reward yourself for a good job. If you go a day without letting negativity bother you, or getting emotionally overstimulated from a minor transgression, buy yourself an ice cream cone. If you did happen to let your emotions control you, you don't get the ice cream cone. Of course the reward doesn't have to be ice cream, that is merely an example of how you should handle the situations.

The reason you should have a rewards system is that it helps you hold yourself accountable. If you had no rewards coming for a job well done, would you be just as eager to do the job right? Most people would not. It helps give you a reason to get better and to discipline yourself.

Rewarding yourself for a job well done also helps you see how far you have come based on a number of times you have been able to reward yourself. This will keep you from being discouraged, and feel like you are making no progress. Remember, staying on the track to being self-disciplined is a discipline all on its own.

3 Make a Commitment

You have to be committed to your goal if you want to get yourself where you want to go. You can't just make a goal with the attitude "If I don't get there, oh well.". You have to make a goal with an "I will do whatever it takes to make that goal" attitude. This is how you go from just a person with a goal, to a person who is going to make a change.

When you make a commitment to be stronger with your emotions, you are making a commitment to having a happier, healthier life. If you want to feel free from emotional chains you have to be more self-disciplined, and not let anyone control your emotions, or let your emotions control you. You have to make a commitment to being in control of your emotions. Without that commitment, you are likely to fall back into your old ways. No one wants to see you fail, and you should not want to see yourself fail. When you make that commitment, make it with every fiber of your being.

It doesn't matter if you tell the world about your goal, or if you keep it to yourself. All that matters is that you make that goal, and you commit to following through with every aspect that will get you to that goal.

Conclusion

Thank you again for your purchase of this book. In this book, you have learned about thought, problem-solving, attention span, learning, and memory. Hopefully, you will use what you have learned to help guide you to success.

Once you have finished this book, put these tips to the test to help yourself become the person you want to be and achieve an uninhibited mind.

THANK YOU

Dear treasured reader, I would like to thank you from the bottom of my heart purchasing this valuable resource on transforming your habits. I sincerely hope the book is able to help you realize your dream of living the life you were meant to live.

I hope you've gotten some valuable information that you can use daily to better your life and those around you as well. If you liked it would you be so kind as to leave an honest/positive review for my book. I would appreciate it very much.

Here's to a happy and better you.

To Your Success,
Jonathan S. Walker

About The Author

Hi there it's Jonathan Walker here, I want to share a little bit about myself so that we can get to know each other on a deeper level. I grew up in California, USA, and have lived there for the better part of my life. I knew I wanted to be able to travel and experience the world the way it was meant to be seen and I've done just that. I've travelled to most places around the world and I'm enjoying every minute of it for sure. In my free time I love to play tennis and believe it or not, compose songs. I wish you all the best again in your endeavours, and may your dreams, whatever they may be, come true abundantly in the near future.

www.ingramcontent.com/pod-product-compliance
Lightning Source LLC
LaVergne TN
LVHW010344070526
838199LV00065B/5787